Decorate with Ribbon

Trendy burlap and other styles of ribbon make quick and easy embellishments for home décor and fashion accessories.

LEISURE ARTS, INC. • Maumelle, Arkansas

Table Décor

SHOPPING LIST

NAPKIN RINGS

- ☐ thin jute cord
- ☐ 7/8"w burlap ribbon (3/4 yard for each flower)
- ☐ craft glue

PLACE MATS

- ☐ place mats
- ☐ 1 1/2"w grosgrain ribbon
- ☐ craft glue

TABLE RUNNER

- ☐ thick jute cord
- ☐ thin jute cord
- ☐ 7/8"w burlap ribbon (3/4 yard for each flower)
- ☐ assorted green ribbons
- ☐ craft glue

To make the napkin rings:

1. Make loop flowers (page 31) with the ribbon, leaving the jute ends 6" long.
2. Tie the flowers to your napkins.

To make the place mats:

Starting at a corner, glue the ribbon to one place mat edge. Fold the ribbon to form a mitered corner and glue to the next edge. Continue around the place mat. Cut and fold under the ribbon end; glue in place.

To make the table runner:

1. Cut a thick jute cord length to lie across the middle of your table. Tie a knot about 2" from each end.
2. Make loop flowers (page 31) with the burlap ribbon, leaving the jute ends 6" long.
3. Cut 8" lengths of the green ribbons. Tie the green ribbons and flowers to the thick jute cord.

Flowered Wreath

SHOPPING LIST

- ☐ 16" dia. foam wreath
- ☐ 5 yards of $2^1/_2$"w white and black ribbon
- ☐ $2^1/_2$ yards of $1^1/_2$"w pink houndstooth wire-edged ribbon
- ☐ $1^1/_2$ yards of $^7/_8$"w blue burlap ribbon
- ☐ 1 yard of $1^1/_2$"w yellow burlap ribbon
- ☐ 1 yard of $1^1/_2$"w green burlap ribbon
- ☐ 1 yard of $1^1/_2$"w pink patterned ribbon
- ☐ 6 buttons for flower centers
- ☐ floral wire
- ☐ sewing needle
- ☐ yellow and green thread
- ☐ craft glue
- ☐ low-temp glue gun and glue sticks

To make the wreath:

Unless otherwise specified, use the low-temp glue gun and glue sticks for all gluing.

1. Wrap the wreath with the white and black ribbon, securing with glue.
2. Make a six-loop pink houndstooth ribbon bow (measuring out 8" for each loop and leaving 8" tails), securing the bow with floral wire. Tie the bow to the wreath with a 22" ribbon length.
3. Make two loop flowers (page 31) with the blue ribbon, using yellow thread to wrap the flower instead of jute. Make two gathered flowers each with the pink patterned ribbon, yellow burlap ribbon, and green burlap ribbon.
4. Glue buttons to the gathered flower centers. Glue the flowers to the wreath.

Ottoman

Nothing could be easier! We picked 6 black and white patterned ribbons (you could use scraps left over from other projects), glued them to the lid of a storage ottoman, and tidied up the ends with a contrasting color ribbon wrap. Now, relax and put your feet up.

Ribbon-Covered Shade

SHOPPING LIST

- ☐ 5" square self-adhesive lampshade
- ☐ assorted ribbons (we used 1 yard each of 5 ribbons)
- ☐ craft glue

To make the lampshade:

1. Cut ribbons 3" longer than the height of the lampshade.
2. Remove the adhesive covering on one side of the shade. Center a ribbon length on the shade and press into the adhesive. Continue around the shade until it is completely covered.
3. Fold the ends to the inside on the bottom and top and glue. Once glue is dry, trim the ends evenly.

Ribbon Stripes Lampshade

SHOPPING LIST

- ☐ fabric-covered lampshade (our shade is 10" dia. x 10"h)
- ☐ 2 coordinating ribbons (we used 4 yards of each)
- ☐ craft glue

To make the lampshade:

1. Cut ribbons 5" longer than the height of the lampshade.
2. Tie two contrasting ribbons around the lampshade, adjusting the knots so they are at the top and bottom of the shade. Continue around the shade, evenly spacing the ribbons. Add a drop or two of craft glue to hold the ribbons in place. Trim the ribbon ends at an angle.

Flowered Pillow Cover

SHOPPING LIST

- ☐ pre-made 16" square pillow cover
- ☐ $1\frac{1}{2}$ yards of $2\frac{1}{2}$"w burlap ribbon
- ☐ three $1\frac{1}{8}$" dia. buttons for flower centers
- ☐ embroidery floss
- ☐ sewing needle and thread
- ☐ craft glue

To make the pillow cover:

1. Make three gathered flowers (page 31).
2. Glue the flowers to the pillow cover. Knot embroidery floss through the buttonholes. Glue the buttons to the flowers.

Burlap Wreath

SHOPPING LIST

- ☐ 16" dia. foam wreath
- ☐ $^{3}/_{4}$ yard of beige fabric
- ☐ 9 yards of $2^{1}/_{2}$"w burlap ribbon to wrap wreath
- ☐ $2^{3}/_{4}$ yards of $2^{1}/_{2}$"w burlap ribbon for bow
- ☐ thick jute
- ☐ 8" high wood letter
- ☐ acrylic paint and paintbrush
- ☐ floral wire
- ☐ floral pins
- ☐ hot glue gun and glue sticks

To make the wreath:

1. Wrap the wreath with 2"w fabric strips, securing with floral pins. Wrap the wreath with the burlap ribbon, securing with floral pins.
2. Make a six-loop bow (measuring out 12" for each loop and leaving 11" tails), securing the bow with floral wire. Attach the bow to the wreath with floral pins. Cut two 72" lengths of thick jute. Holding both lengths together, tie the jute in a bow around the wreath and ribbon bow. Knot the jute ends.
3. Paint the letter and glue to the wreath.

Lighted Vase

SHOPPING LIST

- ☐ cylinder vase (our vase is 6" dia. x 13$^1/_2$"h)
- ☐ 2$^1/_2$"w open-weave ribbon (we used about 3 yards to wrap our vase)
- ☐ patterned ribbon (we used about 2$^1/_4$ yards)
- ☐ silk flowers (we used 4)
- ☐ battery-operated mini lights (available with the bridal crafting supplies)
- ☐ hot glue gun and glue sticks

To make the light:

1. Wrap the open-weave ribbon around the vase, gluing at the top and bottom.
2. Wrap several patterned ribbon lengths around the vase, overlapping and gluing at the front. Glue a flower over each overlapped ribbon point.
3. Place the battery-operated lights in the vase.

Beribboned Pillow Cover

SHOPPING LIST

- ☐ pre-made 16" square pillow cover
- ☐ 17" lengths of assorted ribbons (we used 4 ribbons)
- ☐ $^5/_8$ yard of 17"w paper-backed fusible web
- ☐ water soluble fabric marker
- ☐ aluminum foil
- ☐ pressing cloth
- ☐ fabric glue

To make the pillow cover:

1. Use the fabric marker to lightly mark placement lines for the ribbons.
2. Follow the aluminum foil method (page 32) to adhere the ribbons to the pillow cover, folding the ribbon ends under $^1/_2$". Glue the ends in place.

Ribbon-Trimmed Curtain

SHOPPING LIST

- ☐ curtain panel
- ☐ ribbon lengths that are 4" longer than the curtain panel's width
- ☐ water-soluble fabric marker
- ☐ paper-backed fusible web
- ☐ aluminum foil
- ☐ pressing cloth

To make the curtain:

1. Use the fabric marker to lightly mark placement lines for the ribbons.
2. Follow the aluminum foil method (page 32) to adhere the ribbons to the curtain panel, turning and fusing the cut ends to the back.

Valance

Perk up a window with color-coordinated ribbons and fabric strips. Tear 3$^1/_2$" wide fabric strips, cut several different ribbon lengths, and knot them on a curtain rod. Instant valance!

Tulips

SHOPPING LIST

- ☐ 9" tall milk bottle or vase
- ☐ $2^{1}/_{2}$"w burlap ribbon for bottle
- ☐ $^{3}/_{4}$ yard of 5"w burlap ribbon for each flower
- ☐ thin jute
- ☐ three $^{5}/_{8}$" dia. buttons
- ☐ grassy floral stems with buds
- ☐ 18-gauge paper stem wire
- ☐ floral wire
- ☐ green floral tape
- ☐ hot glue gun and glue sticks

To make the tulips:

1. Glue the $2^{1}/_{2}$"w ribbon to the bottle; fringe the end. Tie a jute length through each button and knot on the back; trim the jute ends. Glue the buttons to the ribbon.
2. To make the petals for each tulip, cut the 5"w burlap ribbon into five 5" lengths. Follow **Figs. 1-4** to complete a petal, wrapping with floral wire to secure. Make five petals.

Fig. 1

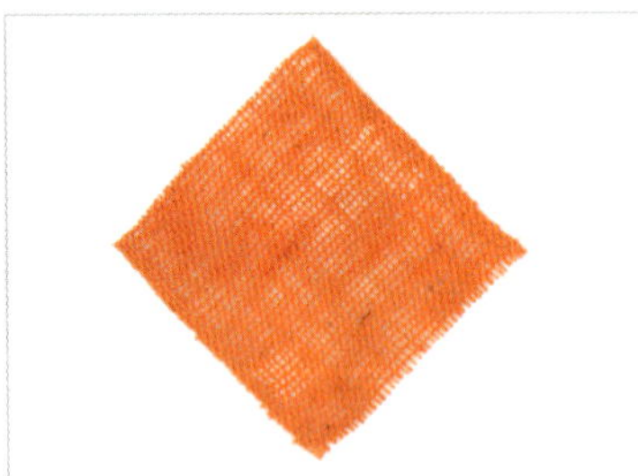

Fig. 2

Fig. 3

Fig. 4

3. For each tulip, curl one end of a stem wire around a pencil to form the stamen. Holding the curled stem in the middle, arrange the petals around the stem and wrap with floral tape ***(Fig. 5)***. Continue wrapping the tape down to the end of the stem. Make three tulips.

Fig. 5

4. Arrange the tulips and grassy stems in the bottle.

Ribbon Canvases

SHOPPING LIST

For each canvas:

- ☐ 12" square artist canvas
- ☐ two 16" squares of colored burlap
- ☐ stapler
- ☐ assorted ribbons in 16" lengths
- ☐ craft glue

To make each canvas:

1. Center the canvas, wrong side up, on a burlap square. Neatly fold the burlap to the canvas wrong side and staple to the canvas frame. Repeat with the remaining burlap square.
2. Position the ribbons on the canvas and spot glue in place. Once the glue is dry, staple the ribbon ends on the canvas back.

Vintage-Look Lampshade

SHOPPING LIST

- ☐ fabric-covered lampshade (our shade is 16" dia. x 10½"h)
- ☐ assorted ribbons (we used about 1½ yards each of 4 ribbons)
- ☐ straight pins
- ☐ craft glue

To make the lampshade:

Beginning on the very bottom of the lampshade, glue the ribbons to the shade, using pins to hold the ribbon in place as the glue dries.

Monogrammed Pillow Cover

SHOPPING LIST

- ☐ pre-made 18" square pillow cover
- ☐ black Sharpie® marker
- ☐ 3/4 yard of 2 1/2"w yellow burlap ribbon
- ☐ 1 yard of 2 1/2"w natural burlap ribbon
- ☐ 2 1/8 yards of 7/8"w orange burlap ribbon
- ☐ three 5/8" dia. buttons for flower centers
- ☐ thin jute
- ☐ sewing needle
- ☐ beige and yellow thread
- ☐ craft glue

To make the pillow cover:

1. Choose a font on your computer and print out the monogram to fit the pillow cover. Our letter is 6" high. Cut out the letter and draw around it on the pillow cover center front. Outline and fill in the letter with the marker.
2. Make 3 pleated flowers (page 31) with the yellow ribbon. Make 2 gathered flowers with the natural ribbon. Make 3 loop flowers with the orange ribbon.
3. Glue the flowers to the pillow cover. Knot jute through the buttonholes. Glue the buttons to the loop flower centers.

Galvanized Planter

SHOPPING LIST

- ☐ galvanized planter
- ☐ $4^{1}/_{2}$"w colored burlap ribbon
- ☐ $2^{1}/_{2}$"w closely-woven burlap ribbon
- ☐ black Sharpie® marker
- ☐ stencil that will fit on $2^{1}/_{2}$"w ribbon
- ☐ spray adhesive
- ☐ hot glue gun and glue sticks

To make the bucket:

1. Cut ribbon lengths to fit around the planter.
2. Spray a light coat of adhesive on the stencil back. Center the stencil on one end of the $2^{1}/_{2}$"w ribbon. Use the marker to fill in the stencil. Repositioning the stencil as necessary, continue the design along the ribbon length.
3. Wrap the wide ribbon around the planter and hot glue in place. Wrap the stencilled ribbon around the planter and hot glue in place.

Purses and Bags

FLOWERED TABLET HOLDER

A length of summery ribbon and a burlap ribbon twisted flower (page 31) with a pearl center are all that's needed to jazz up a functional, but boring, pre-made felt tablet holder. Fabric glue will hold everything in place.

FLOWERED CLUTCH

Accent a pre-made clutch purse with a burlap ribbon twisted flower. The super-easy instructions are on page 31. Once you've got the flower made, fold a bright green ribbon into a leaf shape and glue the flower and leaf to the clutch bag.

DESIGNER-STYLE BAGS

Make a matching designer-style bag and accessory case. Pick up three coordinating ribbons and some solid color quilted bags. Use the aluminum foil method (page 32) to adhere the ribbons to the bags, folding the ribbon ends under $^1/_2$". Secure the ends with fabric glue. Knot ribbons to the zipper pulls and you've got a great gift—for yourself!

Bow Wreath

SHOPPING LIST

- ☐ 16" dia. foam wreath
- ☐ $2^1/_2$ yards of $1^1/_2$"w ribbon to cover wreath edges
- ☐ assorted ribbons for bows (we used 12 different ribbons, about $3^1/_2$ yards of each ribbon)
- ☐ floral wire
- ☐ floral pins

To make the wreath:

1. Pin a $1^1/_2$"w ribbon length around the outer wreath edge. Pin a $1^1/_2$"w ribbon length to the inner wreath edge.
2. Cut the remaining ribbons into 28" lengths. Fold each length into a bow and secure with a 6" floral wire length *(Fig. 1)*.

Fig. 1

3. Pin the bows to the wreath.

Criss-Cross Ribbons Lampshade

SHOPPING LIST

- ☐ lampshade (our shade is 14" dia. x 9"h)
- ☐ $^1/_8$"w and $^1/_{16}$"w satin ribbon (we used about 8 yards of each width ribbon)
- ☐ straight pins
- ☐ craft glue

To make the lampshade:

1. Position lengths of ribbon on the lampshade, pinning at the top and bottom. Try arranging your ribbon at several different angles.
2. Once you are happy with the arrangement, fold the ribbon ends to the shade wrong side and glue in place at the top and bottom.

Ribbon Bowl

SHOPPING LIST

- ☐ assorted ribbons
- ☐ bowl to use as a form
- ☐ craft glue
- ☐ plastic wrap

To make the ribbon bowl:

1. Turn the bowl upside down and cover with plastic wrap.
2. Thin the craft glue with water, using about 2 parts glue to 1 part water. Cut ribbon into assorted lengths. Dip the ribbons in the glue; remove the excess with your fingers. Apply the ribbons to the bowl bottom and sides. Keep adding ribbons until you are happy with the look. Allow to dry completely.
3. Remove the ribbon bowl from the bowl form. Trim ribbon ends as desired.

Monogram

SHOPPING LIST

- ☐ 18" tall wood letter
- ☐ cream spray paint
- ☐ wood-tone spray paint
- ☐ 5/8"w jute ribbon for stripes (we used about 4 yards)
- ☐ 1 3/4 yards of 1 1/2"w wire-edged satin ribbon for twisted flowers
- ☐ 1 yard of 2 1/2"w burlap ribbon for gathered flowers
- ☐ buttons and other embellishments
- ☐ stapler
- ☐ sewing needle and thread
- ☐ craft glue
- ☐ low-temp glue gun and glue sticks

To make the monogram:

Unless otherwise specified, use the low-temp glue gun and glue sticks for all gluing.

1. Working in a well-ventilated area, spray the letter cream. Once dry, lightly spray with wood-tone spray.
2. Position the jute ribbon diagonally on the letter and spot glue in place with craft glue. Wrap the ends to the back of the letter and staple.
3. Make three satin ribbon twisted flowers (page 31). Make two burlap ribbon gathered flowers. Glue buttons to the gathered flower centers.
4. Glue the flowers, buttons, and embellishments to the letter as desired.

General Instructions

GATHERED FLOWER

Cut a 16" length of ribbon. Thread a sewing needle with a doubled thread length. Work Running Stitches close to one long ribbon edge. Pull the thread to gather the ribbon; knot the thread and trim the ends. ***TIP:*** *If your burlap ribbon has a finished edge, try trimming it off and fringing the long edges for a different look.*

LOOP FLOWER

Cut three 8" lengths of 7/8"w ribbon. For each loop, fold a ribbon length into a loop, overlapping the ends about 1/2". Use craft glue to secure the ribbon ends; allow to dry. Overlap the loops in a flower shape and wrap the center with a 12" length of thin jute; knot the jute and trim the ends.

GATHERED FLOWER

LOOP FLOWER

PLEATED FLOWER

Cut an 8" length of ribbon. Accordion pleat the ribbon length. Tightly wrap the pleated center with a matching color doubled thread length; knot the thread and trim the ends.

TWISTED FLOWER

Cut a 20" length of ribbon. Twist one end of the ribbon and curl to begin a spiral. Using a low-temp glue gun, glue the back of the spiral to hold the curl in place. Continue twisting and spiraling, gluing as necessary. Glue the end to the back of the flower.

PLEATED FLOWER

TWISTED FLOWER

ALUMINUM FOIL METHOD TO MAKE FUSIBLE RIBBONS

Place paper-backed fusible web on the ironing board, ***web side up***. Place the ribbons on the fusible web, ***right side up*** *(Fig. 1)*. Completely cover with aluminum foil. Press with an iron and allow to cool. Remove the paper backing and peel the ribbons from the foil. Trim away any stray fusible web. Use a pressing cloth and follow the manufacturer's instructions to fuse the ribbons to the project.

Fig. 1

Production Team: Designer – Patti Wallenfang; Design Assistant – Kelly Reider; Technical Writer – Mary Sullivan Hutcheson; Technical Assistants – Frances Huddleston, Lisa Lancaster, and Jean Lewis; Editorial Writer – Susan Frantz Wiles; Senior Graphic Artist – Lora Puls; Graphic Artists – Jessica Bramlett and Stacy Owens; Photo Stylist – Lori Wenger; Photographers – Jason Masters and Ken West.